What is a Community?

Grades 2-4

Written by Ruth Solski
Illustrated by Brian Hill

W9-ARU-915

ISBN 1-55035-175-3
Copyright 1990
Revised January 2006

Published in the United States by:
On the Mark Press
3909 Witmer Road PMB 175
Niagara Falls, New York
14305
www.onthemarkpress.com

Published in Canada by:
S&S Learning Materials
15 Dairy Avenue
Napanee, Ontario
K7R 1M4
www.sslearning.com

At A Glance™

Learning Expectations	Kinds of Communities	Having Fun in My Community	Community Creative Thinking	Travel in My Community	Working in My Community	My Community	Keep My Community Safe & Clean	Buildings in My Community	Working with Community Words	Researching My Community
Literacy Skills										
• Making Comparisons	•					•				
• Noting Details	•					•				
• Evaluation	•	•	•			•		•		
• Brainstorming		•		•		•	•	•		
• Drawing Conclusions						•				
• Recalling Information	•					•		•		
• Expressing an Opinion				•	•					
• Creative Thinking				•						
• Classifying				•					•	
• Word Recognition									•	
• Seeing Relationships									•	
• Plurals									•	
• Compound Words									•	
• Syllabication									•	
• Capitalization and Punctuation									•	
• Adjectives, Verbs, Nouns									•	
• Alphabetical Order									•	
• Recognizing Vocabulary								•		
Creative Writing										
• Writing an Acrostic Poem			•							
• Writing a Thank You Note			•							
• Good Neighbor Award			•							
• Writing a Community Book			•							
Mathematics Skills										
• Surveying and Graphing				•	•					
Mapping Skills										
• Using a Local Map										•
• Locating Streets										•
Creative Skills										
• Designing a Community Sign										•
• Designing a Community Postcard			•							
• Designing a Community Button/Pin			•							
• Designing a Community Poster			•							
• Designing a Community Flag			•							

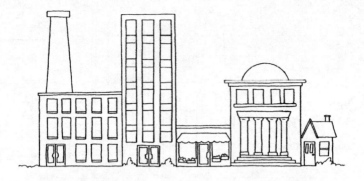

Table of Contents

At A Glance™.. 2

List of Resources 4

List of Vocabulary 6

Aims and Objectives 8

Materials to Collect 8

Teacher Input Suggestions 10

Student Activity Check Sheet 15

Teacher Evaluation Checklist 16

List of Skills 17

Kinds of Communities 19

My Community 27

Having Fun in My Community 42

Keeping My Community Clean 47

Community Creative Thinking 54

Buildings in My Community 63

Travel in My Community 72

Working With Community Words 77

Working in My Community 85

Researching My Community 89

Reproducible Blank Activity Cards 94

Answer Key 96

List of Resources

1. Kalman, Bobbie. Crabtree Publishing Company; c1986

   This is My World Series

   Fun With My Friends
   I Like School
   People at Work
   People at Play
   I Live in a City

   This is an excellent series to use while studying a community.

2. McKay, Roberta & Hobal, Jackie. Globe/Modern Curriculum Press; ©1982

   Can You Tell Where I Live Series

   Exploring Neighborhoods
   Exploring Rural Neighborhoods
   Exploring Town Neighborhoods
   Exploring City Neighborhoods

3. Scanlan, Tom. **Exploring Your Neighbourhood.** IS Five Press, Toronto; ©1984.

4. Bolwell, Laurie & Lines, Cliff. **How Towns Grow and Change.** Wayland Publishers Limited; ©1985.

5. Bolwell, Laurie & Lines, Cliff. **How Towns Work.** Wayland Publishers Limited; ©1985.

6. Knight, Lowry & Richards, Leslie. **Cities Are for People**. Oxford University Press; ©1977.
7. Prelutsky, Jack. **The Random House Book of Poetry**. Random House, New York; ©1983

   In this book there is a section that contains poetry about city life.

8. Moorcroft, Colin. **Homes and Cities**. Franklin Watts; ©1982

9. Arnold, Caroline. **What is a Community?**. Franklin Watts; ©1982

What is a Community?

List of Vocabulary

Community Words

community, neighborhood, country, province, state, space, size, roads, streets, courts, crescents, boulevards, highways, freeways, corner, large, small, people, families, helpers, city, town, village, neighbors, bridges, laws, rules, signs

Kinds of Communities

urban, suburban, rural, fishing, farming, mining, lumbering, industrial, ranching, woodlot, pond, jungle, desert, Arctic, ocean, port, island

Buildings in a Community

homes, houses, apartments, one-storey house, bungalow, two-storey house, townhouse, detached homes, attached homes, condominium, trailer, mobile home, cottage, hotel, motel, factories, store, theaters, skating rink, arena, dome, gas stations, plaza, bowling alley, churches, clinics, hospitals, shopping centers, train station, bus station, town hall, city hall, mosque, synagogue, temple, cathedral, halls, libraries, high-rise, sky scraper, office buildings, warehouses, barns, restaurants, airport, art gallery, museum

Community Transportation

bicycle, walk, car, truck, jeep, bus, subway, street car, trolley, motorcycle, van, tractor, taxi, train, airplane, skidoo, boat, ferry boat, barge

Community Helpers

police officer, fire fighter, mail carrier, postal worker, doctor, lawyer, dentist, nurse, crossing guard, safety patroller, construction worker, carpenter, contractor, electrician, plumber, locksmith, bus driver, taxi driver, baker, chef, sales clerk, waitress, banker, truck driver, printer, painter, teacher, minister, priest, rabbi, garbage collector, principal, custodian, mayor

Community Recreation Areas

schoolyard, playground, park, zoo, community center, pools, arenas, beaches, sports stadium, amusement parks

Community Land Forms

hilly, flat, mountains, forests, woods, ponds, lakes, creeks, streams, ocean, bay, island, desert

Community Communication

telephone, talk, letter, flyers, newspapers, radio, bulletin boards, cards, television, messages, programs, announcements, loud speakers, computers, fax machine

Things People Do in a Community

work, play, shop, travel, worship, build, tear down, visit, manufacture, grow, plant, sell, help, move, live, co-operate, talk, share

People Who May Live in a Community

Canadian, American, Polish, Ukrainian, Russian, French, German, Japanese, Dutch, Chinese, Korean, Jewish, Italian, Portuguese, Mexican, Spanish, Austrian, English, Irish, Scottish, Egyptian, Indian, Swedish, Finnish, Belgian, Black, etc.

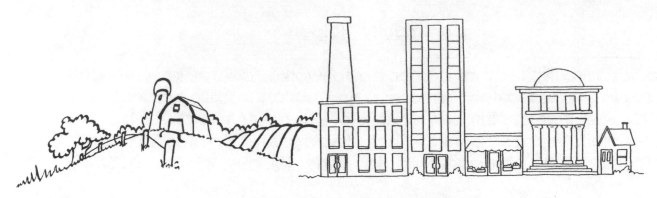

What is a Community?

Aims and Objectives

1. To become aware of the different types of communities in a country.

2. To develop an understanding that all communities have similar characteristics.

3. To identify local landmarks.

4. To understand that a community is made up of many ethnic and cultural groups.

5. To locate the local community on a map of the province or state of a country.

6. To become more familiar with one's community.

What is a Community?

Materials to Collect

- maps of the world, country, province or state, local community

- a large globe

- pictures of the local community, famous landmarks, buildings, people, vehicles, homes, factories

- postcards, calendars, buttons, pennants, banners

- brochures, pamphlets, handbooks

- pictures of different kinds of communities
  e.g.   urban, suburban, rural, fishing, mining, lumbering, farming, industrial, ranching, mountain, animal

- pictures and posters of famous cities

- pictures of the local community in the past

- information on the community's history

- information on the different cultures in your community

- information on and pictures of the community's flag, crest, coat of arms, motto, flower

- magazines, real estate brochures, newspaper ads containing homes and buildings, food, clothing

- obtain a sand table or a large display table for map making

- books related to living in a community, types of communities, different cultures, food, transportation

- collect local newspapers

- look for songs and recordings that have themes about being neighbors, getting along, ethnic music

- look for stories and poetry about communities, friendship, transportation

- related films, filmstrips, videos

Make sure that you check with your school teacher-librarian for some of the resources. Some resources may be obtained from your city or town hall, tourist information center and local historical groups.

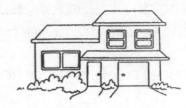

What is a Community?

Teacher Input Suggestions

Note:

Many teacher input sessions should be implemented before the students begin working on the activities. Make sure you give your teacher-librarian plenty of notice that you will be doing a unit with your students on the local community. She/he will need time to collect information, books and pictures. The teacher-librarian may be interested in becoming a partner and can help share the workload and planning.

The following suggestions could be added to your program.

1. Introduce the topic by displaying (on a bulletin board) pictures of urban, suburban and rural communities. Discuss the three types of communities.

2. Develop charts about the three types of communities listing their characteristics. Refer to the pictures frequently noting their similarities and differences. Record your students' observations on the three charts.

Urban	Suburban	Rural
- a city - big buildings	- outside a city - mainly homes	- farms - barns

3. Compare the communities under the following headings:

> a) amount of land
> b) buildings
> c) vehicles
> d) kinds of animals
> e) shopping facilities
> f) plants

4. Discuss the following concepts:

> a) What is a neighborhood?
> b) What is a community?
> c) What is a city?
> d) What is a town?
> e) What is a village?
> f) Why do people live in a community?
> g) What makes a community?
> h) Land forms, bodies of water in the community
> i) Climate - Weather
> j) Community Helpers
> k) Lifestyle in the Community
> l) Recreation in the Community
> m) Shopping Facilities
> n) How the Community is Maintained
> o) Role of the Mayor and the Councillors

5. Locate your country on a map of the world. Using a map of your country locate the province or state in which you live. On a provincial or state map locate the community in which you live. Using a map of your community locate the street on which you live. Also locate main streets and discuss the directions north, south, east and west.

Allow your students to explore the map of the community. They will enjoy finding streets, roads and highways.

Try to display all the maps in one area so that your students will have a better grasp of the concepts: world, country, province or state, community.

6. Explore the immediate neighborhood surrounding the school on a walking tour. Develop a response sheet for the students. On it they will record things that they see on the tour. Make a summary chart when you return to class.

7. Arrange a bus tour of your community. The teacher and parent volunteers could record the students' observations. If you can, have someone take photographs of landmarks and interesting buildings seen on the tour. When they are developed display them on a bulletin board around the charts on which you have recorded the observations made by your students,

   On the following charts record the observations from the tour.

   a) Buildings We Saw
   b) Kinds of Homes
   c) Stores in our Community
   d) Recreation Areas
   e) Vehicles We Saw
   f) People at Work
   g) Factories in our Community

8. Create a table top or sand table model of the local neighborhood.

9. Discuss the different cultural groups in the community. Talk about the names of the students in your class and the ethnic origin of their names. Survey the class to find out if any students were born in a different country, and if their parents or their grandparents were born elsewhere. List the names of the different countries.

10. Once the cultural background of the class has been established plan a series of cultural theme days with the class.

    Suggested Activities:

    a) Invite resource people from various ethnic cultural groups to make presentations about their customs and costumes.

b) Visit a local ethnic cultural center, church or store.

c) Display craft items, dolls, costumes, artifacts from different countries.

d) Participate in folk dances and games from other countries.

e) Read ethnic folk tales and legends.

f) Study art, designs and statues from other countries.

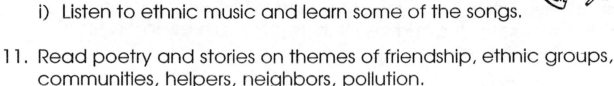

g) Prepare foods that ethnic groups eat.

h) Display books and magazines written in the language of ethnic groups.

i) Listen to ethnic music and learn some of the songs.

11. Read poetry and stories on themes of friendship, ethnic groups, communities, helpers, neighbors, pollution.

12. The following activities could be added to your centers:

a) Classifying man-made things/natural things.

b) Classifying pictures of communities as rural/suburban/urban.

c) Classifying pictures of things that belong in each community on charts.

d) Painting scenes of a community, buildings and homes.

e) Making puppets of community helpers, ethnic children.

f) Making maps of the classroom, school, playground, neighborhood.

13. The ideas and activities in this unit may be used as an introduction and provide a base for you and your students before studying other communities in your country and in other countries.

    The following units are published by S & S Learning Materials Limited and may be used in your classroom.

> A Fishing Community
> A Wheat Farming Community
> A Mining Community
> A Lumbering Community
> A Ranching Community
> An Inuit Community
> Switzerland, A Mountain Community

14. Your local television station may have films or videos of special cultural events that have taken place in your community over the years. Contact them to see if they have anything available pertaining to the community.

15. Perhaps a local historian has slides of famous landmarks that could be shown to the class.

16. Culminate your study of your local community with a community class picnic in a local park. Have your students participate in an ethnic box lunch and a variety of ethnic games and sports.

WHAT IS A COMMUNITY?

Name: _____

In each box print the number of each activity that you have completed.

Kinds of Communities	My Community
Having Fun in My Community	Keeping My Community Safe and Clean
Community Creative Thinking	Buildings in My Community
Travel in My Community	Working With Community Words
Working in My Community	Researching My Community

Teacher Evaluation Checklist

What is a Community?

Name of Student: _____ **Date:** _____

The student can/does

Make Comparisons _____   Survey/Graph _____
Note Details _____   Apply Language Skills _____
Apply Learned Knowledge _____   Research a Given Topic _____
Brainstorm a Given Topic _____   Participate in Class
Think Creatively _____   Discussions _____
Classify _____   Participate in a Group _____

Number of Activities Completed _____

Completion of Activities

Positive Areas of Growth

Areas to Improve

What is a Community?

List of Skills

Kinds of Communities

1. Making Comparisons
2. Noting Details
3. Using Knowledge
4. Illustrating Animal Communities
5. Evaluating

My Community

1. Brainstorming
2. Evaluating
3. Brainstorming
4. Drawing Conclusions
5. Recalling Information
6. Brainstorming
7. Brainstorming
8. Recalling Information
9. Noting Details
10. Making Comparisons
11. Brainstorming
12. Recalling Information
13. Recalling Information
14. Brainstorming
15. Brainstorming

Having Fun In My Community

1. Brainstorming
2. Brainstorming
3. Evaluating
4. Evaluating
5. Brainstorming
6. Evaluating

Keeping My Community Safe and Clean

1. Recalling Knowledge
2. Brainstorming
3. Brainstorming/Evaluating
4. Expressing an Opinion
5. Brainstorming
6. Creative Thinking
7. Brainstorming

Community Creative Thinking

1. Community Acrostic Poem
2. Writing a Thank You Note
3. Designing a Community Poster
4. Community Book
5. Writing a Letter
6. Designing a Community Flag
7. Designing a Button/Pin
8. Community in the Future
9. Designing a Postcard
10. Good Neighbor Award
11. Evaluating/Expressing Opinion

Buildings in My Community

1. Home Survey/Graphing
2. Brainstorming Types of Homes
3. Brainstorming Types of Buildings
4. Brainstorming Building Materials
5. Classifying Helper to Job
6. Matching Building/Word

Travel In My Community

1. Brainstorming Ways We Travel
2. Brainstorming Ways Products Travel
3. Classifying Ways We Travel
4. Surveying Ways We Travel
5. Travel in the Future

Working With Community Words

1. Seeing Relationships
2. Making Words Plural
3. Making Compound Words
4. Syllabication
5. Classifying Words
6. Capitalization/Punctuation
7. Writing Questions
8. Brainstorming Adjectives
9. Brainstorming Verbs
10. Brainstorming Nouns
11. Alphabetical Order

Working In My Community

1. Expressing Opinions
2. Work Survey
3. Researching Parents' Jobs
4. Researching Places of Work

Researching My Community

1. Using a Local Map
2. Using a Local Map
3. Locating Streets
4. Ways People Communicate in a Community
5. Identifying Services
6. Community Flag
7. Community Flower
8. Designing a Community Sign
9. Researching Community History

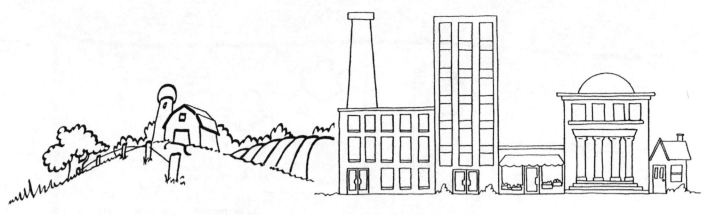

Kinds of Communities #1

Children who live in an urban (city) community and children who live in a farming community would probably do different things to have fun.

Make a list in each box to compare the things that they do every day.

City Child

Farm Child

City Community

KEY

SCHOOL
HOUSE
APARTMENT
OFFICE

BANK
CHURCH
GAS STATION
PARK

SHOPPING
PARKING LOT
CITY HALL

Farming Community

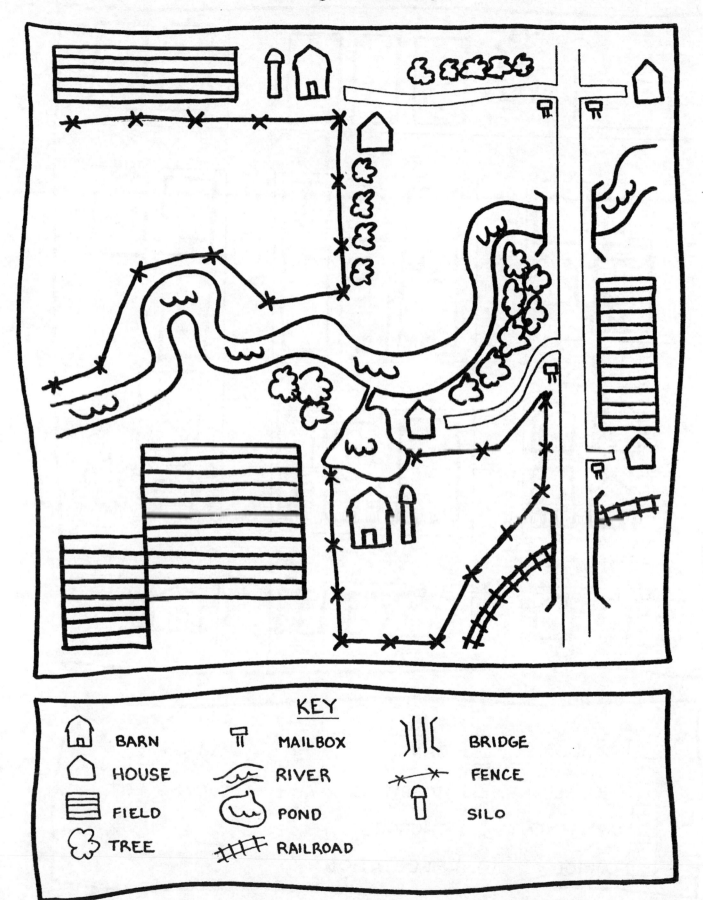

KEY

🏠 BARN   🚏 MAILBOX   )||(BRIDGE

⌂ HOUSE   ～ RIVER   ✕—✕ FENCE

▤ FIELD   ◯ POND   🏛 SILO

🌳 TREE   ⫴⫴ RAILROAD

Town Community

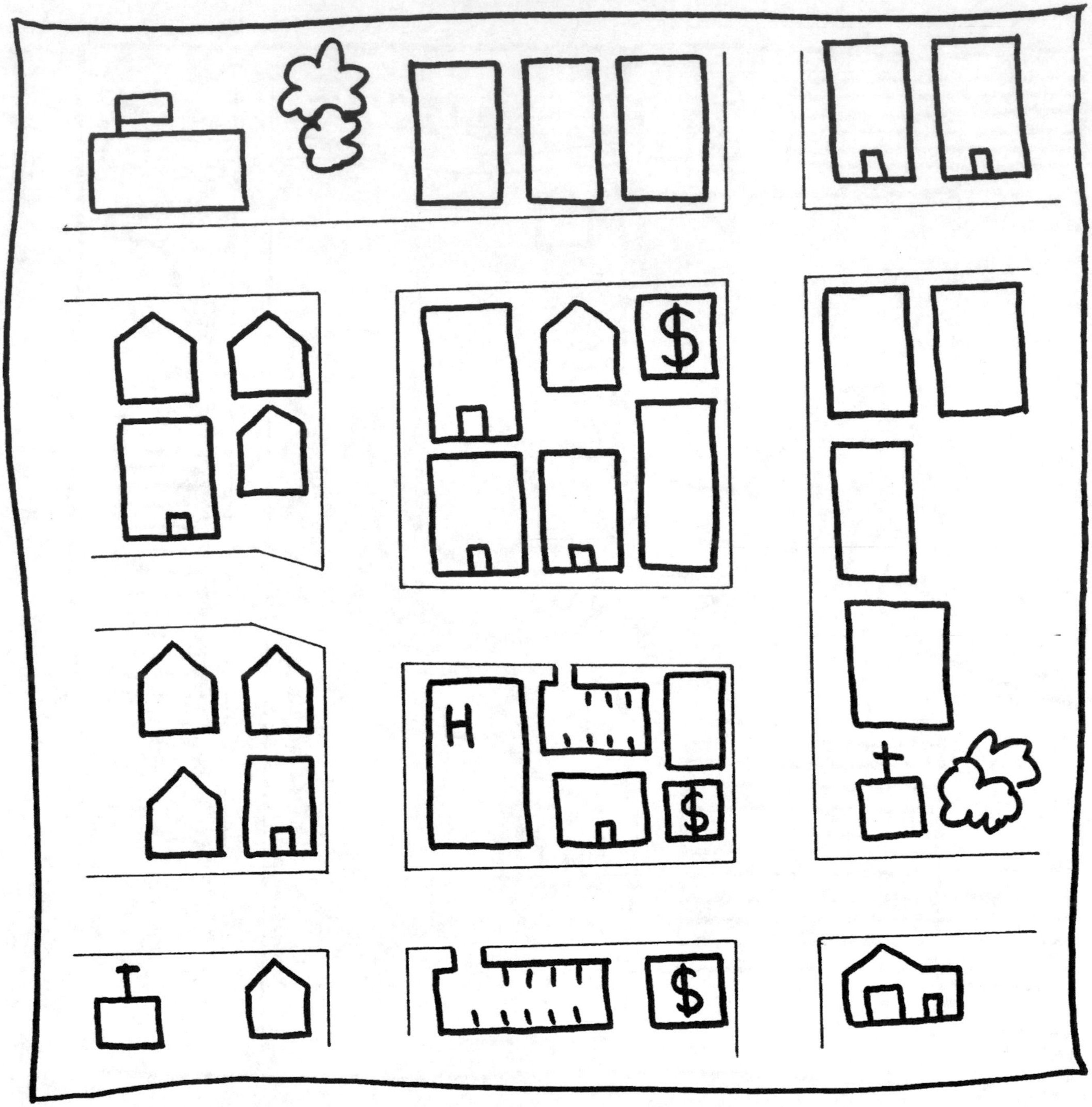

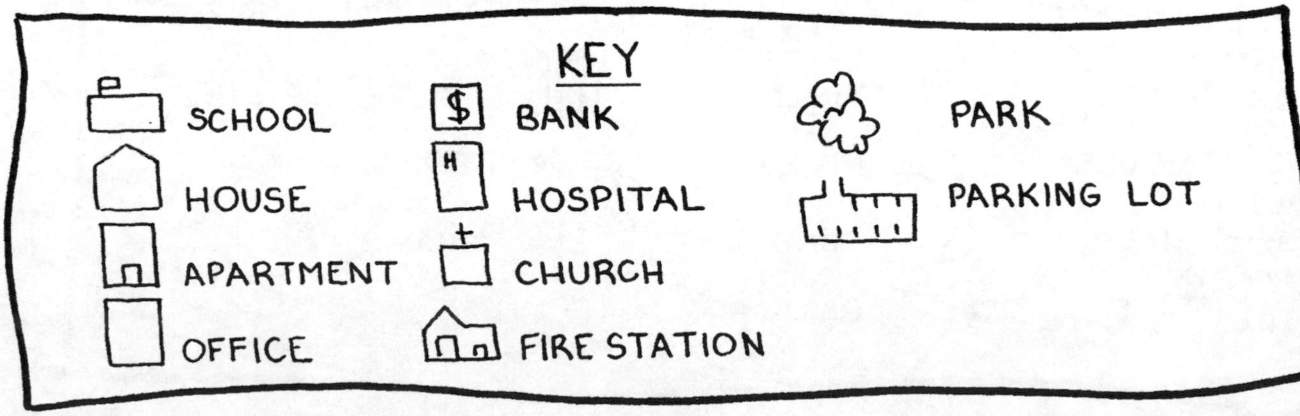
KEY
SCHOOL
HOUSE
APARTMENT
OFFICE
BANK
HOSPITAL
CHURCH
FIRE STATION
PARK
PARKING LOT

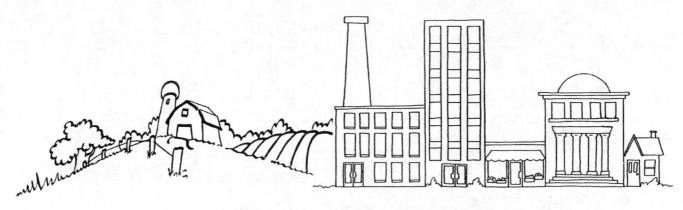

Kinds of Communities #2

Look at the maps of a city, a farm and a town community.

What can you tell about each community? List the things.

City Community

_____

_____

_____

Farm Community

_____

_____

_____

Town Community

_____

_____

_____

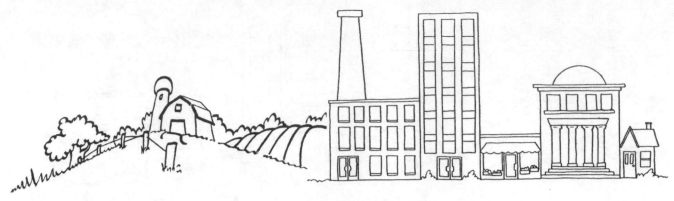

Kinds of Communities #3

There are different kinds of communities in our country.

e.g. Fishing Community   Mining Community
     Lumbering Community   Ranching Community
     Farming Community   Industrial Community

Illustrate a product that you might use that comes from each community.

Fishing Community	Mining Community
Lumbering Community	Ranching Community
Farming Community	Industrial Community

Kinds of Communities #4

Animals live in communities as well as people.

e.g. Pond Community
Woodlot Community
Jungle Community
Desert Community
Arctic Community
Ocean Community

Draw an animal or animals that live in each community.

Pond Community	Jungle Community
Arctic Community	**Woodlot Community**
Desert Community	**Ocean Community**

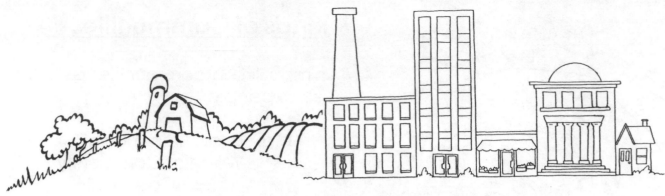

Kinds of Communities #5

Pretend that your family is going to move to another community.

What kind of community would you like it to be? Tell why.

What things would you like your new community to have?

I would like to move to a _____

_____

_____

_____

_____

_____

I hope there are (is) _____

_____

_____

_____

_____

_____

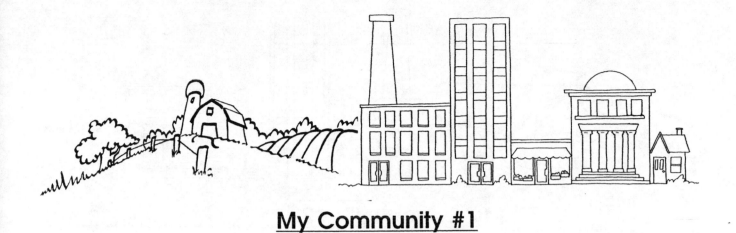

My Community #1

Everyone lives in some kind of a community.

There are often many interesting people, places and things to do in any community.

What would you like to know about your community?

Make up questions that you would like answered.

_____

_____

_____

_____

_____

_____

_____

_____

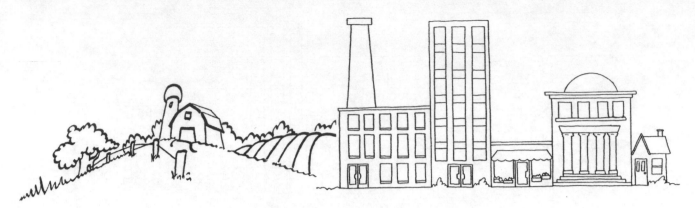

My Community #2

A community is a place where people live together.

Think about your community.

Draw a picture of something that you like about it.

Tell why?

I like the _____

because _____

_____

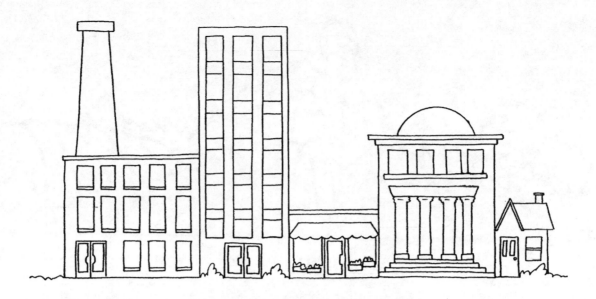

My Community #3

There are many things that make a place a community.

How many things can you think of?

Make a list below.

My community is made up of:

_____

_____

_____

_____

_____

_____

_____

_____

My Community #4

People live in a community for many reasons.

Tell why you think people live in your community.

Try to give three good answers in sentences.

I think people live in my community because .....

_____

_____

_____

_____

_____

_____

_____

_____

My Community #5

There are many communities in a country. Some are big and some are small.

What do you know about your community?

Tell about as many things as you can.

My community is...............

_____

_____

_____

_____

_____

_____

_____

_____

_____

_____

My Community #6

A community is used in many different ways.

e.g. for a place to live

Think of ways that your community is used.

Make a list of the ways.

My community is used for ....

_____

_____

_____

_____

_____

_____

_____

_____

My Community #7

People are an important part of a community.

Some communities have many people while others have only a few people.

How many people live in your community?

What are they like?

Tell all you can about the people in your community.

The people in my community are _____

_____

_____

_____

_____

My Community #8

How well do you know your community?

Can you complete this sheet.

My name is _____ . I am _____

years old. I live at _____
                                    (street address)

My community is called _____
                                    (city, town, village)

My community is west of _____ .
                                    (name of closest place)

_____ is east of my community.
            (name of closest place)

I live in a community that is south of _____ .
                                    (name of closest place)

My community is north of _____ .
                                    (name of closest place)

My community is located in the province (state) called_____

_____ in the country of _____ .

The population of my community is_____ .

The mayor of my community is _____ .

My Community #9

Every community has different land forms.

Some may be near lakes, rivers, streams, mountains or oceans.

What does your community look like?

Does it have a lot of hills?

Is it flat?

Are there any bodies of water near it or running through it?

Are there any mountains and valleys?

What kinds of trees and plants grow there?

Write a story describing the way your community looks.

 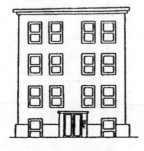 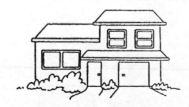

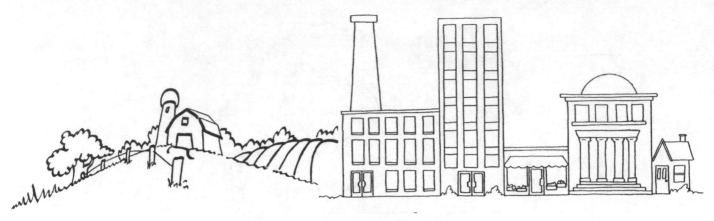

My Community #10

Sounds that you would hear in an urban (city) community would be different from the ones that you would hear in a rural (farming) community.

On a chart like the one below compare the sounds that you would hear in each community.

Sounds Heard

in

An Urban Community	A Rural Community
horns honking	cows mooing

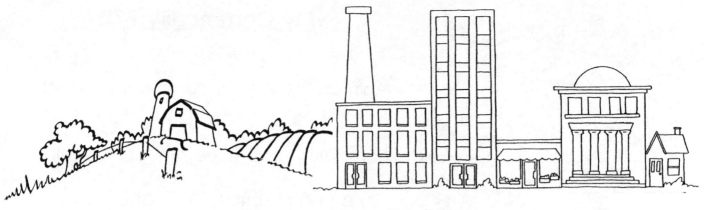

My Community #11

Have you ever taken the time to stop and listen to the different sounds that your community makes?

Turn on your ears and listen!

Make a list of all the sounds that you can hear.

Star the ones that are very loud.

The Sounds of My Community

_____

_____

_____

_____

_____

_____

_____

_____

My Community #12

Animals live in your community as well as people.

Some are tame while others are wild.

On a chart illustrate and label animals that you have seen living in your community.

e.g.

Animals That Live in My Community	
Wild	**Tame**

My Community #13

Some communities are cold while others are hot.

What is the weather like in your community?

1. Name the months of the year when it is the coldest?

   _____

2. Name the months of the year when it is the hottest?

   _____

   _____

3. When does your community get the most rain? Name the season or seasons.

   _____

   _____

4. Does it snow in your community? Tell when.

   _____

   _____

5. When do plants grow in your community?

   _____

   _____

My Community #14

In some communities people must wear different clothes during the year because the weather changes.

Draw how you dress in your community during each season.

Me in the Winter!	Me in the Spring!
Me in the Summer!	**Me in the Fall!**

My Community #15

During the year your community may show changes in how it looks.

In each circle below illustrate the way your community looks during the

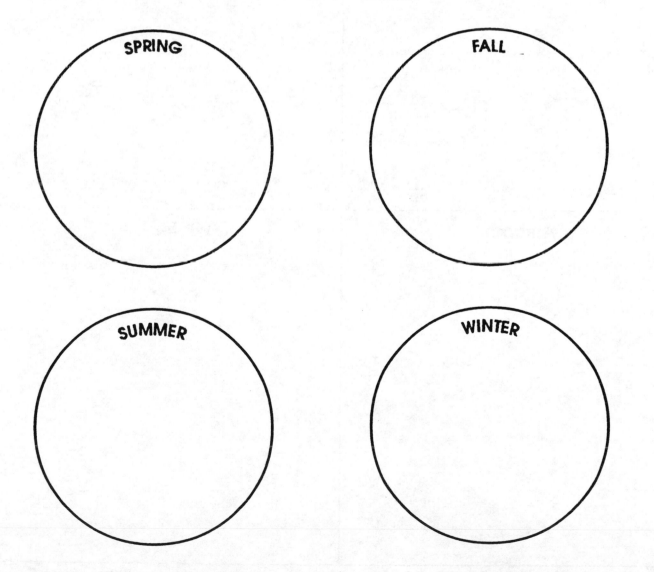

SPRING

FALL

SUMMER

WINTER

Having Fun in My Community #1

During the year you may do different things to have fun.

Draw a picture showing something that you do for fun in the...

Spring	Summer

Autumn	Winter

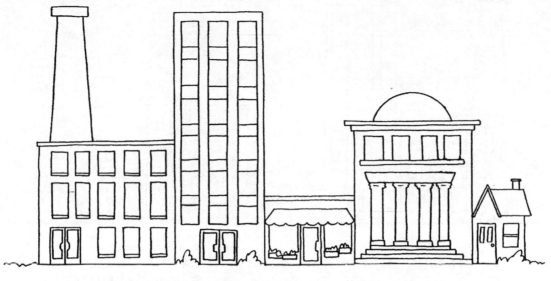

Having Fun in My Community #2

Communities provide people with places where they can enjoy themselves and have fun.

Where do you go to have fun in your community?

In the boxes below draw and label pictures of buildings that you use in your community to have fun.

1. _____	2. _____
3. _____	**4.** _____

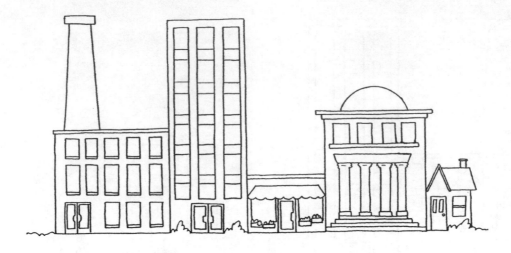

Having Fun in My Community #3

Everyone loves to go out and eat.

Do you have a favorite place to eat in your community?

What foods do you like to eat there?

Draw a picture of your favorite restaurant.

List the foods that you like to eat.

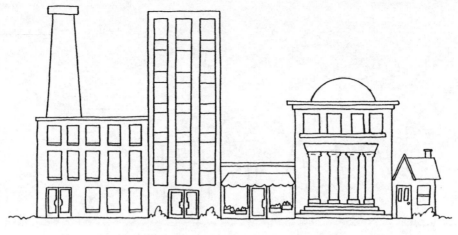

Having Fun in My Community #4

Going shopping in your community can be fun too.

Do you have a favorite store in which you love to shop?

Why is it your favorite?

What kinds of things do you like to buy there?

Illustrate a shopping trip to your favorite store.

Tell all about your trip In a few good sentences.

Having Fun in My Community #5

Where do you like to play with your friends in your neighborhood?

Is it your backyard
        school playground
        neighborhood park
        empty lot?

Draw a picture of you playing with your friends in your favorite place.

In a few good sentences describe the things that you do.

Having Fun in My Community #6

Playing safely in a community is very important.

Can you think of places in your community that are not safe for playing?

Design a safety poster warning children to stay away from a dangerous place in your community.

Keeping My Community Safe and Clean #3

Pollution makes a community ugly.

Look for signs of pollution in your community.

Make a list of signs that you have seen in your community.

How can you help to stop pollution in your community?

List the ways.

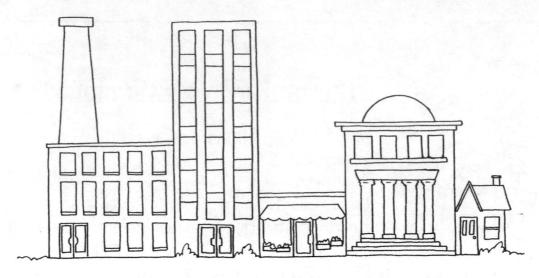

Keeping My Community Safe and Clean #1

Communities have rules called laws.

These rules help to keep our community a safe place to live.

Think of rules that you have in your community.

Write them in a list on a chart like the one below.

Rules for My Community

1. Stop when the traffic light is red.

_____

_____

_____

_____

_____

_____

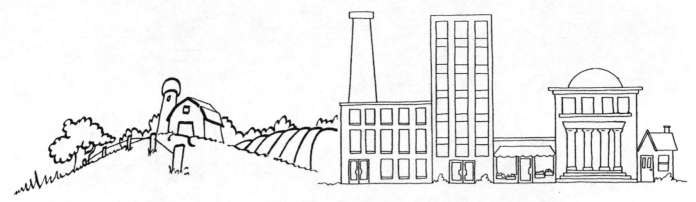

Keeping My Community Safe and Clean #2

Signs are used in a community to remind people to travel and live safely.

Draw signs that you have seen in your community.

Safety Signs

Keeping My Community Safe and Clean #4

The air and water in a community is often polluted by smoke and chemicals that come from factories.

Is there a factory in your community that causes pollution?

If so, write a letter to the factory owner telling him/her how you feel about the pollution.

Send it by mail.

I hope you get an answer.

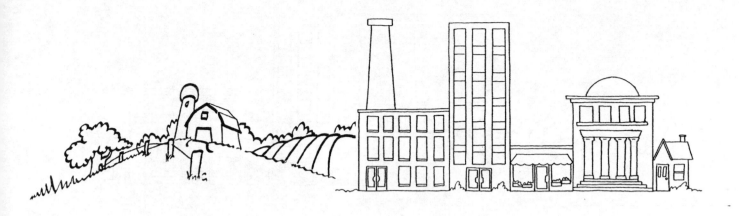

Keeping My Community Safe and Clean #5

All communities have laws or rules.

Think of reasons why they are important to have.

_____

_____

_____

_____

_____

Can you suggest a new law or laws that your community should have?

_____

_____

_____

_____

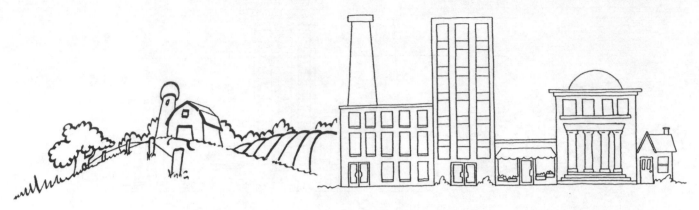

Keeping My Community Safe and Clean #6

A community looks more attractive and inviting when it is kept clean.

Think of ways people in your community can keep it clean.

Design a poster to remind them to help keep their community a better looking place to live.

e.g.

Keep Boston Clean!

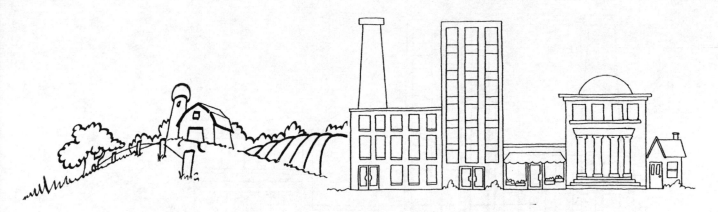

Keeping My Community Safe and Clean #7

Communities have helpers who keep our communities safe and clean.

Some helpers take away your garbage or put out fires or clean the streets.

Who are the helpers in your community?

Illustrate and label as many as you can on a chart.

e.g.

HELPERS IN MY COMMUNITY

The Police Officer

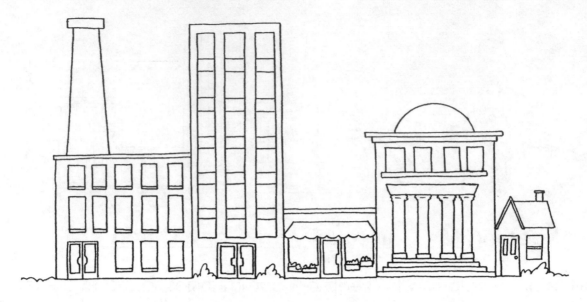

Community Creative Thinking #1

Write an acrostic poem about your community.

Print the name of your community vertically.

Begin each line of your poem with a word that begins with the same letter in its name.

e.g.

> **B**oston is a big city,
>
> **O**ld and Historical,
>
> **S**teadily growing bigger.
>
> **T**ourists come to visit it,
>
> **O**n their summer vacations.
>
> **N**ice place to visit and live.

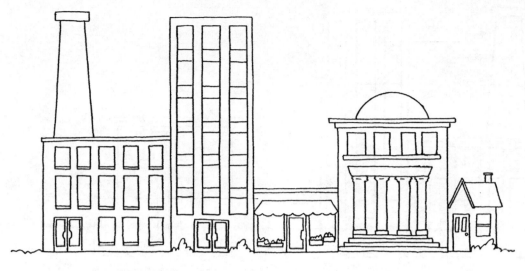

Community Creative Thinking #2

Community helpers work hard to keep our community a safe and clean place to live.

Write a thank you note to any community helper who you feel does a good job.

e.g.

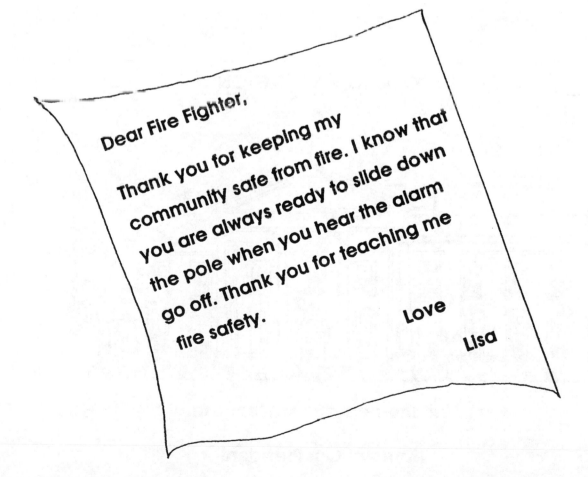

Dear Fire Fighter,

Thank you for keeping my community safe from fire. I know that you are always ready to slide down the pole when you hear the alarm go off. Thank you for teaching me fire safety.

Love
Lisa

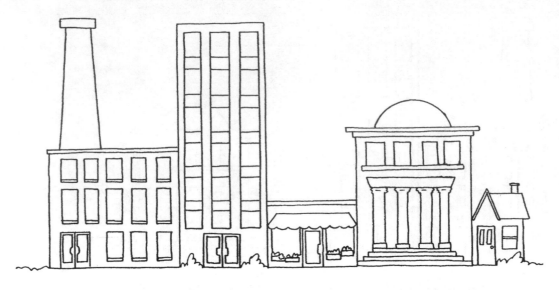

Community Creative Thinking #3

Your community is a great place to live.

Design a poster that you would put up telling people about it.

Print an interesting sentence under the picture.

e.g.

COME TO WASHINGTON

Visit the beautiful Whitehouse!

Home of Our President

Community Creative Thinking #4

Pretend that you are a local author.

Create a book about your community.

In your book draw pictures of any of the things that you would see in your community.

Write a few sentences about each picture.

Things you could include are:

Important Buildings	**Things People Do**
Places People Work	**Kinds of People**
Famous Places	**Things That You Like**

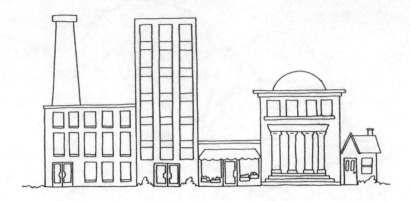

Community Creative Thinking #5

The mayor of your city is the person people in your community pick to help run it. He or she has a very important job.

Write a letter to your mayor telling him or her how you feel about your community.

Perhaps there are ways that your community could be better.

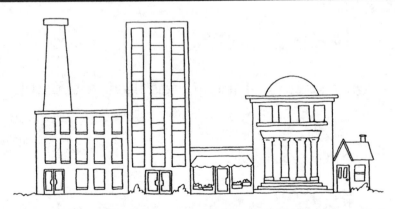

Community Creative Thinking #6

Design a flag for your community.

What colors will you make it?

What symbol can you put on it that will represent your community?

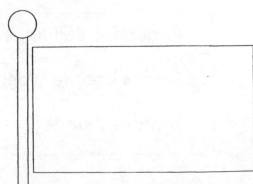

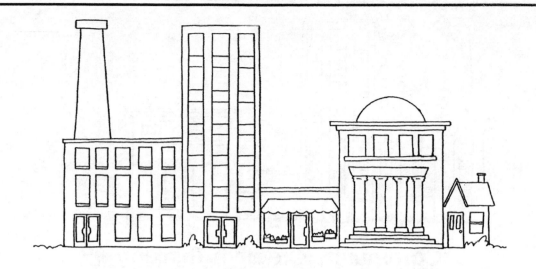

Community Creative Thinking #7

When you visit a different community people will often give out a pin or button that represents it.

Design a pin or button for your own community.

Community Creative Thinking #8

Communities are always changing.

People move away, people move in, buildings are being torn down and new buildings are being built.

Look into the future!

How do you think your community will look in one hundred years.

Paint a picture of your community in the future.

Write a description of it.

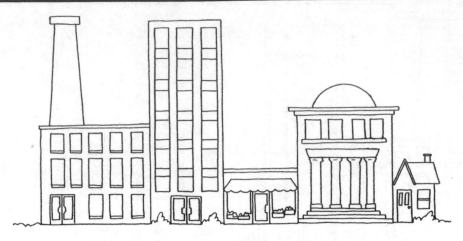

Community Creative Thinking #9

Most communities sell picture postcards of landmarks in their community.

Design a picture postcard for your community.

Which important place or building will you illustrate on it?

Attach the instruction card to an envelope.

Buildings in My Community #6

In the envelope are some picture cards of buildings that you may see in your community and cards with their names.

Match the picture to its name card.

e.g.

| house |

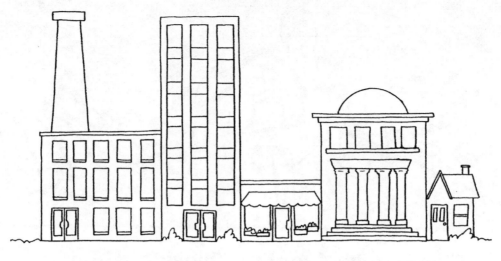

Community Creative Thinking #10

Some people in a community work hard to keep their homes looking nice.

Look around your neighborhood.

Is there a neighbor who keeps his home and yard in good condition and makes your street look attractive?

Design a certificate to give to that neighbor.

e.g.

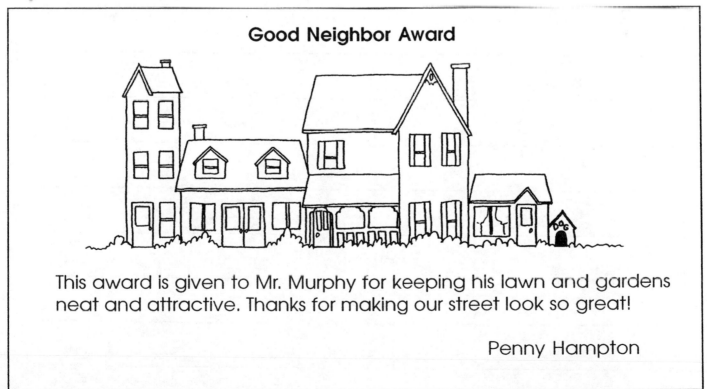

Good Neighbor Award

This award is given to Mr. Murphy for keeping his lawn and gardens neat and attractive. Thanks for making our street look so great!

Penny Hampton

Community Creative Thinking #11

People who live in a community are usually proud of it for many reasons.

Are you proud of your community?

In a few good sentences tell why you are proud to live there.

I am proud of _____

because _____

_____

_____

_____

_____

_____

_____

_____

_____

  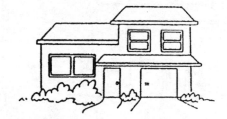

Buildings in My Community #1

People live in different types of homes in a community.

Survey your classmates to find out the kind of house each one lives in.

Kind of Home	Check	Total
1. One Storey		
2. Two Storey		
3. Town House		
4. Split Level		
5. Apartment		
6. Condominium		
7. Semi-detached		
8. Other		

The most popular type of home in our community is

_____

Make a bar graph to show the results of your survey.

Buildings in My Community #2

Communities can have many types of homes.

e.g. apartments
       one storey homes
       two storey homes

What kinds of homes do you have in your community?

Illustrate and label as many kinds as you can on a chart.

e.g.

```

        HOMES IN MY COMMUNITY




```

 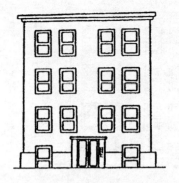 

Buildings in My Community #3

Large and small buildings are seen in a community. Some of them are places where people live, work, play or shop.

What kinds of buildings does your community have?

List their names on a chart.

e.g.

Buildings in My Community

Factories

_____   _____

_____   _____

_____   _____

_____   _____

_____   _____

_____   _____

_____   _____

_____   _____

Buildings in My Community #4

It takes many different types of materials to build a building.

What kinds of materials would you need to build a new building in your community?

Make a list of the materials that you would have to buy.

Buildings in my community are made of:

wood		
nails		

Buildings in My Community #5

It takes many different kinds of workers to build a building or home.

If you were going to build a new building in your community who would you hire?

List the names of the helpers and tell what their jobs would be on a chart.

Helpers	Type of Job
Carpenter	builds the frame of the building

Buildings in My Community #6: Color, cut out and mount the pictures and word cards on a sturdy backing and laminate. Store the cards in an envelope. The student will match the picture to the word.

one storey house	two storey house	semi-detached house
townhouse	apartment house	split-level house
mobile home	cottage	hospital
shopping center	police station	city hall
barn	gas station	library
factory	school	store
fire hall	restaurant	arena
museum	post office	hotel

Travel in My Community #1

People in a community travel about in many different ways.

e.g. walk, ride bicycles

How do the people in your community travel?

Illustrate and label as many ways as you can on a chart.

e.g.

Ways We Travel

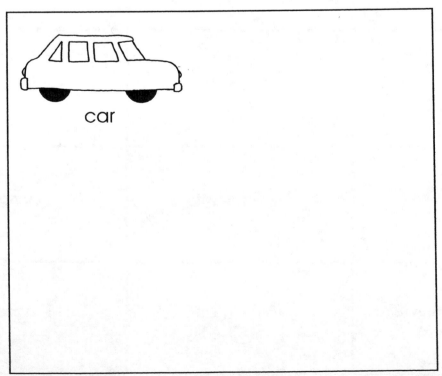

car

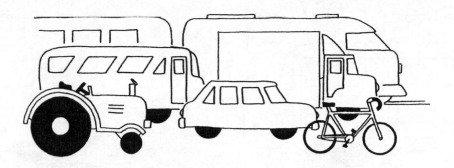

Travel in My Community #2

Everyday products are being brought into a community and also sent out to other communities.

How do products such as food, cars, oil and many others travel in and out of your community.

Make a list of all the possible ways they are transported.

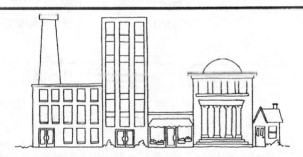

Working With Community Words #3

Match the words in the box to make community compound words.

town	air	ware	high
school	sub	play	air
country	house	port	way
house	yard	ground	plane
side			

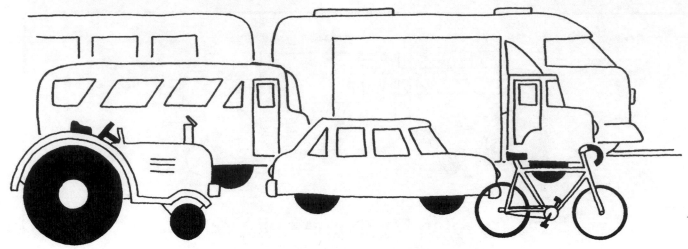

Travel in My Community #3

In a community we can travel on land, on water, underground and in the air.

On the chart, classify the following ways that we travel:

bus   automobile   tractor   truck   helicopter
motor boat   motorcycle   train   van   subway
taxi   balloon   jeep   bicycle   airplane
ferryboat   feet   horse   street car   skidoo
tricycle

Land	Air
Underground	**Water**

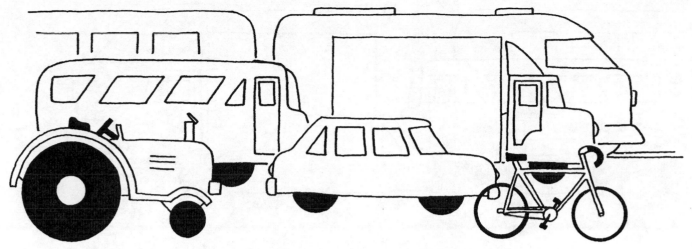

Travel in My Community #4

How do your classmates travel from place to place in your "community?

Survey your classmates to find out the types of vehicles they have used.

Vehicle	Checks	Total
1. tractor		
2. automobile		
3. skidoo		
4. bus		
5. subway		
6. street car		
7. truck		
8. Other		

The vehicle used the most was _____ .

Make a bar graph to show your results.

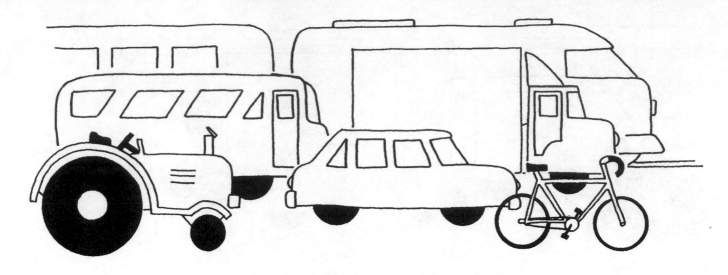

Travel in My Community #5

How do you think the people in your community will travel in the year 2100?

Design four new ways that you may travel by:

Air	Land
Water	**Underground**

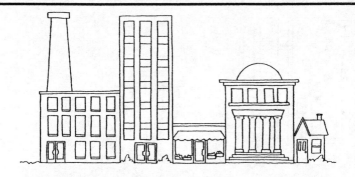

Working With Community Words #1

Copy each group of words below.

Underline the word in each group that doesn't belong.

1. city, town, ocean, village

4. car, van, airplane, taxi

2. apartment, hospital, house, trailer

5. dentist, doctor, plumber, nurse

3. library, hospital, hotel, bridge

6. shop, telephone, store, plaza

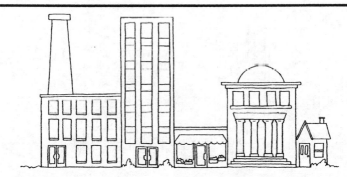

Working With Community Words #2

Large communities have **subways** running under the ground.

The word "subways" is a plural word.

Copy the words below. Beside each one print its plural.

1. factory
2. community
3. bus
4. church

5. library
6. country
7. taxi
8. city

9. village
10. town

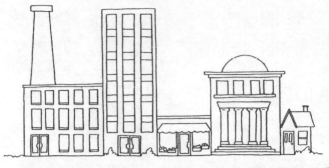

Working With Community Words #4

"Community" is a four syllable word.

Copy the words below. Beside each one print the number of syllables that you hear.

1. condominium
2. neighborhood
3. highway
4. motorcycle

5. ferry
6. library
7. park
8. factories

9. streets
10. hotel

Working With Community Words #6

A sentence is a group of words that tells one idea.

Write three **good** sentences about your community.

Remember:

Begin each sentence with a capital letter and end it with a period.

Try to spell all the words correctly.

  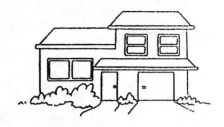

Working With Community Words #5

Classify the following words.

Print **B** for building
V for vehicle
H for helper

1. apartment _____

2. police officer _____

3. electrician _____

4. barn _____

5. factory _____

6. museum _____

7. van _____

8. plumber _____

9. bicycle _____

10. post office _____

11. truck _____

12. transport _____

13. library _____

14. city hall _____

15. automobile _____

16. fire fighter _____

17. carpenter _____

18. cottage _____

19. warehouse _____

20. mail carrier _____

21. store _____

22. bus _____

Working With Community Words #7

Pretend that you are going to interview the mayor of your community.

Think of three good questions that you would ask about his or her job.

Write your questions in good sentences.

Remember to put a capital letter at the beginning and a question mark at the end of each sentence.

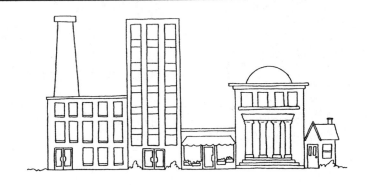

Working With Community Words #8

Some of the buildings in a community are **tall**.

"Tall" is a word that is called an **adjective**. It describes the buildings.

Think of words that you could use to describe the buildings, places and sights in your community.

Complete this list:

tall		
large		
busy		

Working With Community Words #9

Some people in a community **ride** to work on a bus.

The word "ride" is called a verb. A verb is an action word.

Think of ways people and things move about in your community.

Complete this list:

walk _____   _____   _____

drive _____   _____   _____

run _____   _____   _____

_____   _____   _____

_____   _____   _____

_____   _____   _____

_____   _____   _____

_____   _____   _____

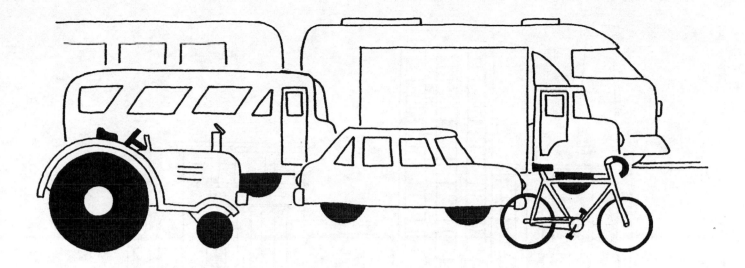

Working With Community Words #10

Trucks and **cars** travel on many community streets.

The words "trucks" and "cars" are nouns.

A noun is a word that names a person, place or thing.

In the box below circle all the nouns.

house	bang	river	arena
walk	police	hospital	pollute
ride	bus	honked	hilly
mayor	live	apartment	travel
factory	lake	friendly	town
fly	people	shopping	library
river	crashes	store	nurse

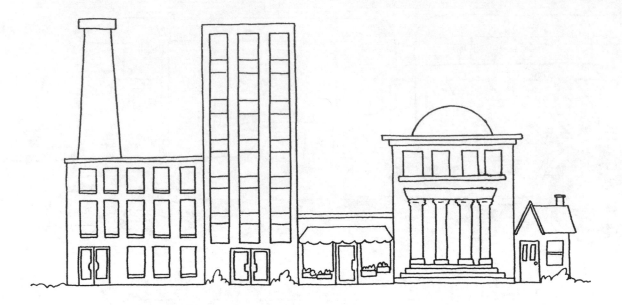

Working With Community Words #11

There are many things to see in your community.

Make your own "Community Alphabet Book".

Illustrate pictures of things that begin with each letter of the alphabet.

e.g.

My Community

A B C

Book

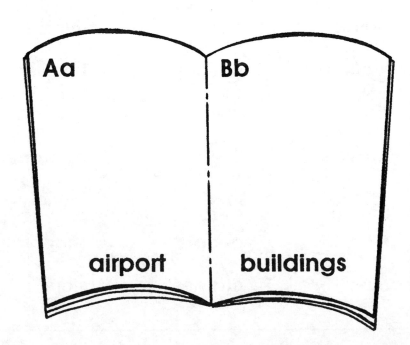

Aa

Bb

airport

buildings

Working in My Community #1

People must go to work for many reasons.

Give some reasons why you think people work.

_____

_____

_____

_____

If people didn't go to work in your community what do you think it would be like? Describe it?

_____

_____

_____

_____

Working in My Community #2

Where do the parents of your classmates work?

Do they work inside or outside of your community?

Survey the class to find out:

Parents Who Work Inside the Community _____

Parents Who Work Outside the Community _____

List the different occupations of your classmates' parents.

_____

_____

_____

_____

_____

_____

_____

_____

Working in My Community #3

What do your parents do every day at work?

Where do they work?

Do they like their jobs?

Interview your parents to find out more about their jobs or careers.

Would you like to do the same type of work? Explain your answer.

_____

_____

_____

_____

_____

_____

_____

_____

Working in My Community #4

In a community there are many places where people might work.

Look in the Yellow Pages of the telephone book and find out the names of five

Stores	Factories
_____	_____
_____	_____
_____	_____
_____	_____
Restaurants	**Other**
_____	_____
_____	_____
_____	_____
_____	_____

Researching My Community #1

Visit the resource center (library) and find a map of your community.

Look at the map carefully. Find the names of ten different streets. Print them neatly.

Have you ever been on any of them?

Star the ones on which you have traveled.

Researching My Community #2

Locate a map of your community in the resource center (library).

Copy down the names of ten interesting streets.

Rewrite the list in alphabetical order.

Researching My Community #3

Streets in a community may be named after famous people, animals, flowers, trees and even the weather.

Look at a map of your community.

Try to find a street that is:

1. a royal name _____

2. an Irish name _____

3. named after a saint _____

4. named after an animal _____

5. named after a bird _____

6. a tree's name _____

7. a Native name _____

8. a girl's name _____

9. the name of a famous person _____

10. the name of a flower _____

Researching My Community #4

If you wanted to find out about events that are happening in your community, how would you find out?

Research to find out the ways in which people communicate in your community.

List at least six possible ways.

Circle the one that you think is the best way.

Researching My Community #6

Does your community have a flag flying in front of your town or city hall?

If it has find out what it looks like.

Illustrate your community's flag.

Researching Your Community #5

Find out where you would go in your community if you:

1. needed to buy food _____

2. wanted to eat out _____

3. needed medicine _____

4. broke a leg _____

5. felt sick _____

6. saw an accident _____

7. saw a burning house _____

8. found a stray dog _____

9. needed gas _____

10. wanted to see a movie _____

11. wanted to meet the mayor _____

12. wanted to borrow a book _____

13. wanted to look at old things _____

14. wanted to look at famous paintings _____

15. wanted to swim _____

16. wanted to learn to skate _____

17. mail a letter _____

18. had a toothache _____

19. wanted to stay overnight _____

20. had to fly to another community _____

Researching My Community #7

Some communities choose a flower for a symbol.

Does your community have a flower as a symbol?

Find out its name and what it looks like.

Illustrate your community's flower.

Researching My Community #8

Many cities have a motto written on its city sign.

THE FRIENDLY CITY

Design a sign for your community.

Make up a motto for it.

Researching My Community #9

Every community has a history.

Try to find out the following things about your community.

1. How old is your community?

2. How did it get its name?

3. Who named it?

4. How has it changed over the years?

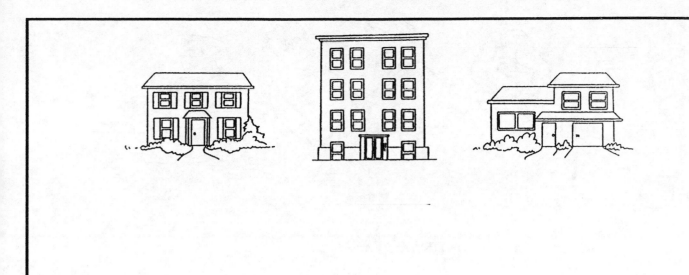

Answer Key

Working With Community Words #1:

1. ocean   2. hospital   3. bridge   4. airplane   5. plumber
6. telephone

Working With Community Words #2:

1. factories   2. communities   3. buses   4. churches   5. libraries
6. countries   7. taxis   8. cities   9. villages   10. towns

Working With Community Words #3:

1. (5)   2. (3)   3. (2)   4. (4)   5. (2)
6. (3)   7. (1)   8. (3)   9. (1)   10. (2)

Working With Community Words #5:

1. B   2. H.   3. H   4. B   5. B   6. B   7. V   8. H   9. V
10. B   11. V   12. V   13. B   14. B   15. V   16. H   17. H   18. B
19. B   20. H   21. B   22. V

Working With Community Words #10:

Nouns: house, river, arena, police, hospital, bus, mayor, apartment, factory, lake,
town, people, library, store, nurse

Publication Listing

See Dealer or
www.onthemarkpress.com
For Pricing
1-800-463-6367

Code #	Title and Grade
OTM-1492	Abel's Island NS 4-6
OTM-1131	Addition & Subtraction Drills Gr. 1-3
OTM-1128	Addition Drills Gr. 1-3
OTM-2504	Addition Gr. 1-3
OTM-14174	Adv. of Huckle Berry Finn NS 7-8
OTM-293	All About Dinosaurs Gr. 2
OTM-102	All About Mexico Gr. 4-6
OTM-120	All About the Ocean Gr. 5-7
OTM-249	All About the Sea Gr. 4-6
OTM-261	All About Weather Gr. 7-8
OTM-2110	All Kinds of Structures Gr. 1
OTM-601	Amazing Aztecs Gr. 4-6
OTM-1468	Amelia Bedelia NS 1-3
OTM-113	America The Beautiful Gr. 4-6
OTM-1457	Amish Adventure NS 7-8
OTM-602	Ancient China Gr. 4-6
OTM-618	Ancient Egypt Gr. 4-6
OTM-621	Ancient Greece Gr. 4-6
OTM-619	Ancient Rome Gr. 4-6
OTM-1453	Anne of Green Gables NS 7-8
OTM-14162	Arnold Lobel Author Study Gr. 2-3
OTM-1622	Australia B/W Pictures
OTM-105	Australia Gr. 5-8
OTM-14224	Banner in the Sky NS 7-8
OTM-401	Be Safe Not Sorry Gr. P-1
OTM-1409	Bear Tales Gr. 2-4
OTM-14202	Bears in Literature Gr. 1-3
OTM-1440	Beatrix Potter Gr. 2-4
OTM-14129	Beatrix Potter: Activity Biography Gr. 2-4
OTM-14257	Because of Winn-Dixie NS Gr. 4-6
OTM-14114	Best Christmas Pageant Ever NS Gr. 4-6
OTM-14107	Borrowers NS Gr. 4-6
OTM-1463	Bridge to Terabithia NS Gr. 4-6
OTM-2524	BTS Numeración Gr. 1-3
OTM-2525	BTS Adición Gr. 1-3
OTM-2526	BTS Sustracción Gr. 1-3
OTM-2527	BTS Fonética Gr. 1-3
OTM-2528	BTS Leer para Entender Gr. 1-3
OTM-2529	BTS Uso de las Mayúsculas y Reglas de Puntuación Gr. 1-3
OTM-2530	BTS Composición de Oraciones Gr. 1-3
OTM-2531	BTS Composici13n de Historias Gr. 1-3
OTM-14256	Bud, Not Buddy NS Gr. 4-6
OTM-1807	Building Word Families L.V. 1-2
OTM-1805	Building Word Families S.V. 1-2
OTM-14164	Call It Courage NS Gr. 7-8
OTM-1467	Call of the Wild NS Gr. 7-8
OTM-2507	Capitalization & Punctuation Gr. 1-3
OTM-14198	Captain Courageous NS Gr. 7-8
OTM-14154	Castle in the Attic NS Gr. 4-6
OTM-631	Castles & Kings Gr. 4-6
OTM-1434	Cats in Literature Gr. 3-6
OTM-14212	Cay NS Gr. 7-8
OTM-2107	Cells, Tissues & Organs Gr. 7-8
OTM-2101	Characteristics of Flight Gr. 4-6
OTM-1466	Charlie and Chocolate Factory NS Gr. 4-6
OTM-1423	Charlotte's Web NS Gr. 4-6
OTM-109	China Today Gr. 5-8
OTM-1470	Chocolate Fever NS Gr. 4-6
OTM-14241	Chocolate Touch NS Gr. 4-6
OTM-14104	Classical Poetry Gr. 7-12
OTM-811	Community Helpers Gr. 1-3
OTM-14183	Copper Sunrise NS Gr. 7-8
OTM-1486	Corduroy and Pocket Corduroy NS Gr. 1-3
OTM-234	Creatures of the Sea Gr. 2-4
OTM-14208	Curse of the Viking Grave NS 7-8
OTM-1121	Data Management Gr. 4-6
OTM-253	Dealing with Dinosaurs Gr. 4-6
OTM-14105	Dicken's Christmas NS Gr. 7-8
OTM-1621	Dinosaurs B/W Pictures
OTM-216	Dinosaurs Gr. 1
OTM-14175	Dinosaurs in Literature Gr. 1-3
OTM-2106	Diversity of Living Things Gr. 4-6
OTM-1127	Division Drills Gr. 4-6
OTM-287	Down by the Sea Gr. 1-3
OTM-1416	Dragons in Literature Gr. 3-6
OTM-2109	Earth's Crust Gr. 6-8
OTM-1612	Egypt B/W Pictures
OTM-14255	Egypt Game NS Gr. 4-6
OTM-628	Egyptians Today and Yesterday Gr. 2-3
OTM-2108	Electricity Gr. 4-6
OTM-285	Energy Gr. 4-6
OTM-2123	Environment Gr. 4-6
OTM-1812	ESL Teaching Ideas Gr. K-8
OTM-14258	Esperanza Rising NS Gr. 4-6
OTM-1822	Exercises in Grammar Gr. 6
OTM-1823	Exercises in Grammar Gr. 7
OTM-1824	Exercises in Grammar Gr. 8
OTM-620	Exploration Gr. 4-6
OTM-1054	Exploring Canada Gr. 1-3
OTM-1056	Exploring Canada Gr. 1-6
OTM-1055	Exploring Canada Gr. 4-6
OTM-820	Exploring My School and Community Gr. 1
OTM-1639	Fables B/W Pictures
OTM-1415	Fables Gr. 4-6
OTM-14168	First 100 Sight Words Gr. 1
OTM-14170	Flowers for Algernon NS Gr. 7-8
OTM-14128	Fly Away Home NS Gr. 4-6
OTM-405	Food: Fact, Fun & Fiction Gr. 1-3
OTM-406	Food: Nutrition & Invention Gr. 4-6
OTM-2118	Force and Motion Gr. 1-3
OTM-2119	Force and Motion Gr. 4-6
OTM-14172	Freckle Juice NS Gr. 1-3
OTM-14209	Giver, The NS Gr. 7-8
OTM-1114	Graph for all Seasons Gr. 1-3
OTM-1490	Great Expectations NS Gr. 7-8
OTM-14169	Great Gilly Hopkins NS Gr. 4-6
OTM-14238	Greek Mythology Gr. 7-8
OTM-2113	Growth & Change in Animals Gr. 2-3
OTM-2114	Growth & Change in Plants Gr. 2-3
OTM-2104	Habitats Gr. 4-6
OTM-14205	Harper Moon NS Gr. 7-8
OTM-14136	Hatchet NS Gr. 7-8
OTM-14184	Hobbit NS Gr. 7-8
OTM-14250	Holes NS Gr. 4-6
OTM-1848	How To Give a Presentation Gr. 4-6
OTM-14125	How To Teach Writing Through 7-9
OTM-1810	How To Write a Composition 6-10
OTM-1809	How To Write a Paragraph 5-10
OTM-1808	How To Write an Essay Gr. 7-12
OTM-1803	How To Write Poetry & Stories 4-6
OTM-407	Human Body Gr. 2-4
OTM-402	Human Body Gr. 4-6
OTM-605	In Days of Yore Gr. 4-6
OTM-606	In Pioneer Days Gr. 2-4
OTM-241	Incredible Dinosaurs Gr. P-1
OTM-14177	Incredible Journey NS Gr. 4-6
OTM-14100	Indian in the Cupboard NS Gr. 4-6
OTM-14193	Island of the Blue Dolphins NS 4-6
OTM-1465	James & The Giant Peach NS 4-6
OTM-1625	Japan B/W Pictures
OTM-106	Japan Gr. 5-8
OTM-1461	Julie of the Wolves NS Gr. 7-8
OTM-502	Junior Music for Fall Gr. 4-6
OTM-505	Junior Music for Spring Gr. 4-6
OTM-506	Junior Music Made Easy for Winter Gr. 4-6
OTM-14140	Kids at Bailey School Gr. 2-4
OTM-298	Learning About Dinosaurs Gr. 3
OTM-1122	Learning About Measurement Gr. 1-3
OTM-1119	Learning About Money USA Gr. 1-3
OTM-1123	Learning About Numbers Gr. 1-3
OTM-269	Learning About Rocks and Soils Gr. 2-3
OTM-1108	Learning About Shapes Gr. 1-3
OTM-2100	Learning About Simple Machines Gr. 1-3
OTM-1104	Learning About the Calendar Gr. 2-3
OTM-1110	Learning About Time Gr. 1-3
OTM-1450	Legends Gr. 4-6
OTM-14130	Life & Adv. of Santa Claus NS 7-8
OTM-210	Life in a Pond Gr. 3-4
OTM-630	Life in the Middle Ages Gr. 7-8
OTM-2103	Light & Sound Gr. 4-6
OTM-14219	Light in the Forest NS Gr. 7-8
OTM-1446	Lion, Witch & the Wardrobe NS 4-6
OTM-1851	Literature Response Forms Gr. 1-3
OTM-1852	Literature Response Forms Gr. 4-6
OTM-14233	Little House on the Prairie NS 4-6
OTM-14109	Lost in the Barrens NS Gr. 7-8
OTM-14167	Magic School Bus Gr. 1-3
OTM-14247	Magic Treehouse Gr. 1-3
OTM-278	Magnets Gr. 3-5
OTM-403	Making Sense of Our Senses K-1
OTM-294	Mammals Gr. 1
OTM-295	Mammals Gr. 2
OTM-296	Mammals Gr. 3
OTM-297	Mammals Gr. 5-6
OTM-14160	Maniac Magee NS Gr. 4-6
OTM-119	Mapping Activities & Outlines! 4-8
OTM-117	Mapping Skills Gr. 1-3
OTM-107	Mapping Skills Gr. 4-6
OTM-2116	Matter & Materials Gr. 1-3
OTM-2117	Matter & Materials Gr. 4-6
OTM-1609	Medieval Life B/W Pictures
OTM-1413	Mice in Literature Gr. 3-5
OTM-14180	Midnight Fox NS Gr. 4-6
OTM-1118	Money Talks – Gr. 3-6
OTM-1497	Mouse & the Motorcycle NS 4-6
OTM-1494	Mr. Poppers Penguins NS Gr. 4-6
OTM-14201	Mrs. Frisby & Rats NS Gr. 4-6
OTM-1826	Multi-Level Spelling USA Gr. 3-6
OTM-1132	Multiplication & Division Drills 4-6
OTM-1130	Multiplication Drills Gr. 4-6
OTM-114	My Country! The USA! Gr. 2-4
OTM-1437	Mystery at Blackrock Island NS 7-8
OTM-14157	Nate the Great and Sticky Case NS Gr. 1-3
OTM-110	New Zealand Gr. 4-8
OTM-1475	Novel Ideas Gr. 4-6
OTM-14244	Number the Stars NS Gr. 4-6
OTM-2503	Numeration Gr. 1-3
OTM-14220	One in Middle Green Kangaroo NS Gr. 1-3
OTM-272	Our Trash Gr. 2-3
OTM-2121	Our Universe Gr. 5-8
OTM-286	Outer Space Gr. 1-2
OTM-118	Outline Maps of the World Gr. 1-8
OTM-1431	Owls in the Family NS Gr. 4-6
OTM-1452	Paperbag Princess NS Gr. 1-3
OTM-212	Passport to Australia Gr. 4-5
OTM-1804	Personal Spelling Dictionary Gr. 2-5
OTM-503	Phantom of the Opera Gr. 6-9
OTM-14171	Phoebe Gilman Author Study Gr. 2-3
OTM-2506	Phonics Gr. 1-3
OTM-1448	Pigs in Literature Gr. 2-4
OTM-1499	Pinballs NS Gr. 4-6
OTM-634	Pirates Gr. 4-6
OTM-2120	Planets Gr. 3-6
OTM-1874	Poetry Prompts Gr. 1-3
OTM-1875	Poetry Prompts Gr. 4-6
OTM-624	Prehistoric Times Gr. 4-6
OTM-501	Primary Music for Fall Gr. 1-3
OTM-504	Primary Music for Spring Gr. 4-6
OTM-507	Primary Music Made Easy for Winter Gr. 1-3
OTM-1120	Probability & Inheritance Gr. 7-10
OTM-1426	Rabbits in Literature Gr. 2-4
OTM-1444	Ramona Quimby Age 8 NS 4-6
OTM-2508	Reading for Meaning Gr. 1-3
OTM-14234	Reading with Arthur Gr. 1-3
OTM-14200	Reading with Curious George 2-4
OTM-14230	Reading with Eric Carle Gr. 1-3
OTM-14251	Reading with Kenneth Oppel 4-6
OTM-1427	Reading with Mercer Mayer 1-2
OTM-14142	Reading with Robert Munsch 1-3
OTM-14225	River NS Gr. 7-8
OTM-508	Robert Schumann-Life & Times Gr. 6-9
OTM-265	Rocks & Minerals Gr. 4-6
OTM-14103	Sadako and 1 000 Paper Cranes NS Gr. 4-6
OTM-404	Safety Gr. 2-4
OTM-1442	Sarah Plain & Tall NS Gr. 4-6
OTM-1601	Sea Creatures B/W Pictures
OTM-279	Sea Creatures Gr. 1-3
OTM-1464	Secret Garden NS Gr. 4-6
OTM-2502	Sentence Writing Gr. 1-3
OTM-1430	Serendipity Series Gr. 3-5
OTM-1866	Shakespeare Shorts – Performing Arts Gr. 2-4
OTM-1867	Shakespeare Shorts – Performing Arts Gr. 4-6
OTM-1868	Shakespeare Shorts – Language Arts Gr. 2-4
OTM-1869	Shakespeare Shorts – Language Arts Gr. 4-6
OTM-14181	Sight Words Activities Gr. 1
OTM-299	Simple Machines Gr. 4-6
OTM-2122	Solar System Gr. 4-6
OTM-205	Space Gr. 2-3
OTM-1834	Spelling Blacklines Gr. 1
OTM-1835	Spelling Blacklines Gr. 2
OTM-1814	Spelling Gr. 1
OTM-1815	Spelling Gr. 2
OTM-1816	Spelling Gr. 3
OTM-1817	Spelling Gr. 4
OTM-1818	Spelling Gr. 5
OTM-1819	Spelling Gr. 6
OTM-1827	Spelling Worksavers #1 Gr. 3-5
OTM-2125	Stable Structures & Mechanisms 3
OTM-14139	Stone Fox NS Gr. 4-6
OTM-14214	Stone Orchard NS Gr. 7-8
OTM-1864	Story Starters Gr. 1-3
OTM-1865	Story Starters Gr. 4-6
OTM-1873	Story Starters Gr. 1-6
OTM-2509	Story Writing Gr. 1-3
OTM-2111	Structures, Mechanisms & Motion 2
OTM-14211	Stuart Little NS Gr. 4-6
OTM-1129	Subtraction Drills Gr. 1-3
OTM-2505	Subtraction Gr. 1-3
OTM-2511	Successful Language Pract. Gr. 1-3
OTM-2512	Successful Math Practice Gr. 1-3
OTM-2309	Summer Learning Gr. K-1
OTM-2310	Summer Learning Gr. 1-2
OTM-2311	Summer Learning Gr. 2-3
OTM-2312	Summer Learning Gr. 3-4
OTM-2313	Summer Learning Gr. 4-5
OTM-2314	Summer Learning Gr. 5-6
OTM-14159	Summer of the Swans NS Gr. 4-6
OTM-1418	Superfudge NS Gr. 4-6
OTM-108	Switzerland Gr. 4-6
OTM-115	Take a Trip to Australia Gr. 2-3
OTM-2102	Taking Off With Flight Gr. 1-3
OTM-1455	Tales of the Fourth Grade NS 4-6
OTM-1472	Ticket to Curlew NS Gr. 4-6
OTM-14222	To Kill a Mockingbird NS Gr. 7-8
OTM-14163	Traditional Poetry Gr. 7-10
OTM-1481	Tuck Everlasting NS Gr. 4-6
OTM-14126	Turtles in Literature Gr. 1-3
OTM-1427	Unicorns in Literature Gr. 3-5
OTM-617	Viking Age Gr. 4-6
OTM-14206	War with Grandpa NS Gr. 4-6
OTM-2124	Water Gr. 2-4
OTM-260	Weather Gr. 4-6
OTM-1417	Wee Folk in Literature Gr. 3-5
OTM-808	What is a Community? Gr. 2-4
OTM-262	What is the Weather Today? 2-4
OTM-1473	Where the Red Fern Grows NS 7-8
OTM-1487	Where the Wild Things Are NS 1-3
OTM-14187	Whipping Boy NS Gr. 4-6
OTM-14226	Who is Frances Rain? NS Gr. 4-6
OTM-509	Wolfgang Amadeus Mozart Gr. 6-9
OTM-14213	Wolf Island NS Gr. 1-3
OTM-14221	Wrinkle in Time NS Gr. 7-8